Macbeth

WILLIAM SHAKESPEARE

Level 4

Retold by Anne Collins
Series Editors: Andy Hopkins and Jocelyn Potter

Pearson Education Limited
Edinburgh Gate, Harlow,
Essex CM20 2JE, England
and Associated Companies throughout the world.

ISBN 0 582 82999 2

The edition first published by Penguin Books 2004

3 5 7 9 10 8 6 4

Set in 11/14pt Bembo
Printed in China
SWTC/03

Produced for the Publishers by Bluestone Press, Charlbury, Oxfordshire, UK

Published by Pearson Education Limited in association with
Penguin Books Ltd, both companies being subsidiaries of Pearson Plc

For a complete list of the titles available in the Penguin Readers series please write to your local
Pearson Education office or to: Marketing Department, Penguin Longman Publishing,
Edinburgh Gate, Harlow, Essex CM20 2JE.

Contents

Introduction

'I have committed so many bloody crimes now that I cannot return to the person I used to be.'

Macbeth is about the fall of a fine man who has one terrible weakness – his political ambition. At the start of the play, Macbeth is a brave soldier who is loved, admired and completely trusted by Duncan, the wise and noble King of Scotland. But then he meets three witches who predict that he will be king, and he starts to think about murdering Duncan. Macbeth sinks deeper and deeper into crime; by the end of the play he has become a lonely tyrant, who is hated by everyone.

Lady Macbeth, Macbeth's wife, is a very dangerous woman. She is even more ambitious than her husband, and has a stronger character. When she hears about the witches' predictions, her only desire is for Macbeth to be king. While Macbeth is unsure about their murderous plans, his wife will not give up. She coldly plans the details of Duncan's murder, while pretending to welcome him as hostess. She calls her husband a coward and a fool as she pushes him down the road to crime.

Macbeth is a very interesting and difficult part for an actor. His character is complicated and changes during the play. Even after he commits terrible acts, we still feel sorry for him. The part of beautiful, ambitious Lady Macbeth is a dream for many actresses. She has murderous plans, but can seem so sweet and innocent to others.

Macbeth is one of Shakespeare's greatest and most powerful plays. It was first printed in 1623, and the story takes place six centuries earlier, in eleventh-century Scotland. But we are still interested today in the effects of ambition; in loyalty and betrayal; in fate, the supernatural and the battle between good and evil. It is also a very exciting play, with sword fights, murders, a ghost and witches. There are few main characters and a strong, simple story that is easy to read, or watch, and to remember.

William Shakespeare, the most famous writer of plays in the English language, was born in Stratford-upon-Avon on 26 April 1564 and died on 23 April 1616. He wrote thirty-seven plays and many poems. Several of his historical plays, like *Macbeth*, are about political ambition and the battle for power.

Macbeth was probably first performed in 1606 for King James I, the first king of both England and Scotland. James was very interested in the subject of witches, although he was afraid of them as well. Shakespeare took the story from a book called *Holinshed's Chronicles*, and the material in the play is not historically correct. But many of the places are real: Macbeth's castle is in Inverness, in the north of Scotland, and Macduff's castle is in the area of Fife, further south.

There have been many interesting and unusual productions of *Macbeth* in different countries, on film and on stage. *Joe Macbeth* (1955) was a Hollywood gangster film, and *Throne of Blood* (1957) was a Japanese film about the battle for power among nobles in Japan in the past. In 1971 the director Roman Polanski made an excellent film of *Macbeth*, which is filmed against a real Scottish background but also uses special effects for the supernatural.

In British theatres, some actors and stage workers believe that it is unlucky to call the play by its name. When *Macbeth* is in production, they call it 'the Scottish play'!

Reading and acting the play

You can read *Macbeth* silently, like every other story in a book. You will have to imagine the places, the characters' clothes and their voices from the words on the page. You can also read it in a group with other people and bring the characters to life by the way you speak the words. You can make them sound angry, sad or afraid, and add silences and important noises, like the knocking at the gate after Duncan's murder or the ringing of the bell. You can also stop and discuss the play. Do the characters mean what they say, or are they hiding their real intentions and feelings?

But *Macbeth* was written for actors on a theatre stage. Sword fights and murders, and the behaviour of unusual supernatural characters like witches and a ghost, are fun to act. The characters can speak through their words, but also through their actions: Macbeth must show his terror of Banquo's ghost at the dinner; Lady Macbeth shows her guilty feelings by trying to wash imaginary blood from her hands; poor Lady Macduff must show her love for her son.

The play moves quickly, so scenes must change quickly too. You will need simple furniture like a table for some scenes in the castles, and pictures or models of trees for the outside forest scenes. You will also have to think about how characters dress. Macbeth wears armour at the beginning and end of the play, but when he becomes king he wears a crown. What should eleventh-century noblewomen like Lady Macbeth and Lady Macduff wear? Are the witches going to be dressed in traditional black clothes? And the ghost will need a lot of blood! You will also need stage equipment – swords, daggers and the witches' magic pot.

The story of *Macbeth* will really come alive through acting. Act it if you can, or read it, but enjoy it!

The Characters in the Play

DUNCAN, King of Scotland
MALCOLM, Duncan's son
DONALBAIN, Duncan's son
MACBETH, Thane of Glamis
LADY MACBETH, wife of Macbeth
SEYTON, Macbeth's servant
SERVANT, Lady Macbeth's servant
BANQUO, thane, friend of Macbeth
FLEANCE, Banquo's son
MACDUFF, Thane of Fife
LADY MACDUFF, wife of Macduff
SON OF MACDUFF
LENNOX
ROSS
MENTETH } Scottish thanes
ANGUS
CATHNESS
SEYWARD, Lord of Northumberland
AN ENGLISH SOLDIER
A CAPTAIN
A DOCTOR
A GATEKEEPER
AN OLD MAN
THREE WITCHES
THREE MURDERERS
A SOLDIER, TWO CHILDREN, EIGHT KINGS (characters shown by the witches)
LORDS, GENTLEMEN, OFFICERS, SOLDIERS, ATTENDANTS, MESSENGERS, SERVANTS

Act 1   The Three Witches

Scene 1   A dark forest

[*It is a wild and stormy night, with thunder and lightning. The three witches enter.*]

FIRST WITCH: When shall we three meet again?
In thunder, lightning or in rain?
SECOND WITCH: When the fighting has ended. When the battle's been lost and won.
THIRD WITCH: That will be before the sun goes down.
FIRST WITCH: Where shall we meet?
SECOND WITCH: On the moor.
THIRD WITCH: We'll meet Macbeth there.
ALL: Good is evil, and evil is good.
Let's fly off through the foggy wood.

[*They leave.*]

Scene 2   An open road in the country

[*King Duncan, Malcolm, Donalbain and Lennox enter from one side with their attendants. An army captain, bleeding, enters from the other side.*]

DUNCAN [*to his sons*]: Who is this man, covered in blood? From his appearance, he can give us the latest news of the battle.
MALCOLM: This officer fought very bravely to stop the enemy taking me prisoner. Hail, brave friend! Tell the King how the battle was going when you left.
CAPTAIN: It was not clear which side was winning. Then brave Macbeth cut a path through the enemy soldiers with his sword

until he came face to face with their cruel leader, Macdownald. He cut him open from his chin to his stomach, and fixed his head on the castle walls.

DUNCAN [*admiringly*]: How brave and noble Macbeth is!

CAPTAIN: But as the enemy were starting to run away, the King of Norway saw a new opportunity to attack us. He brought in fresh soldiers and the battle began again.

DUNCAN: Did that not shock our captains, Macbeth and Banquo?

CAPTAIN: No, not at all. They started to attack the enemy twice as enthusiastically. [*holding his side in pain*] But I am weak; I need help.

DUNCAN: Your words show your true character as clearly as your bleeding cuts. [*to his attendants*] Take him away and fetch doctors for him. [*The captain leaves with the attendants. The Thanes★ of Ross and Angus enter.*] Who is this?

MALCOLM: The noble Thane of Ross.

LENNOX: He is certainly in a hurry. He seems to have some important news to tell us.

ROSS: God save the King!

DUNCAN: Where have you come from, noble Thane?

ROSS: From Fife, great King. The King of Norway was attacking us with great numbers of men, helped by that most disloyal traitor, the Thane of Cawdor. But Macbeth faced him without fear and fought him, and finally the victory was ours.

DUNCAN: That is wonderful news! But the Thane of Cawdor will not betray us again. Go and order his immediate execution. And give his title to Macbeth.

ROSS: I will make sure that it is done.

DUNCAN: He has lost what noble Macbeth has won.

[*They all leave.*]

★ Thane: a Scottish lord

Scene 3   A wild moor

[*The three witches enter to the sound of thunder.*]

FIRST WITCH: Where have you been, sister?

SECOND WITCH: Killing pigs.

THIRD WITCH: And you, sister?

FIRST WITCH: A sailor's wife was eating sweets. 'Give me some,' I said. 'Get away from me, you old witch!' she replied. But she'll be sorry. Her husband's a ship's captain and he's sailed to Aleppo. I'll follow him and start a horrible storm.

[*A drum sounds in the distance.*]

THIRD WITCH: A drum, a drum! Macbeth is coming!

[*They join hands and dance round in a circle. Macbeth and Banquo enter.*]

MACBETH: I have never known such an eventful day.

BANQUO [*seeing the witches and stopping in surprise*]: Who are these creatures, so old and dressed so strangely? They don't look human. [*to the witches*] Are you real? You look like women, but not like normal women.

MACBETH: Speak if you can! Who are you?

FIRST WITCH: Hail, Macbeth! Hail, Thane of Glamis!

SECOND WITCH: Hail, Macbeth! Hail, Thane of Cawdor!

THIRD WITCH: Hail, Macbeth, who will be king one day!

BANQUO [*to Macbeth*]: Why, sir, do you look so surprised, and seem to be afraid of such a wonderful future? [*to the witches*] You've completely silenced my friend with your predictions of noble titles and royal hopes. But you haven't said anything to me. If you really can look into the future, then tell me. I'm not asking for your help and I'm not afraid of your hate.

FIRST WITCH: Hail!

3

'Banquo and Macbeth, hail!'

SECOND WITCH: Hail!

THIRD WITCH: Hail!

FIRST WITCH: You'll be less than Macbeth, but also greater.

SECOND WITCH: Not so happy, but much happier.

THIRD WITCH: Your children will be kings, although *you* won't be king. So hail, Macbeth and Banquo!

FIRST WITCH: Banquo and Macbeth, hail!

[*The witches start to leave.*]

MACBETH [*following*]: Wait! Tell me more! I know that I'm the Thane of Glamis. I got that title when my father died. But how can I be Thane of Cawdor? The Thane of Cawdor is alive and well. And it's unbelievable that I could be king. Where did you get this information, and why have you stopped us on this wild moor to tell us your strange predictions?

[*The witches laugh and disappear.*]

BANQUO: Where have they gone?

MACBETH: Into the air. They seemed real, but they have disappeared like breath in the wind. Why did they not stay?

BANQUO: Were they really here? Or did we imagine it? Have we gone mad?

MACBETH [*laughing*]: Your children will be kings.

BANQUO [*laughing too*]: *You* will be king.

MACBETH: And Thane of Cawdor too, did they not say?

BANQUO: That is what they said. [*calling*] Who is there?

[*Ross and Angus enter.*]

ROSS: The King was very pleased to hear the news of your victory, Macbeth. You put yourself in great personal danger among the enemy soldiers. Messenger after messenger reported how bravely you defended Scotland. So, as a reward, the King has ordered me to give you the title of Thane of Cawdor.

BANQUO [*very surprised*]: What! Are these evil creatures able to predict the truth?

MACBETH [*disbelieving*]: But the Thane of Cawdor is alive. Why are you calling me by another man's title?

ANGUS: The man with that title is still alive, but he is going to be executed. He does not deserve to live. I do not know whether he supported the King of Norway, or our enemy Macdownald, but he betrayed his own country.

MACBETH [*to himself*]: I am the Thane of Glamis, and now of Cawdor too. That was the first step. [*to Ross and Angus*] Thank you for your trouble. [*to Banquo*] Are you not hoping now that your children will be kings? That is what those same creatures promised you.

BANQUO: If that is the direction of your thoughts, then you will start to think about being king. But it is very strange how, when evil creatures want to hurt us, they often tell us the truth about unimportant things. They want to make us trust them. Then it will be easy for them to harm us later. [*to Ross and Angus*] Can I have a word with you, friends?

[*Banquo, Ross and Angus walk away from Macbeth.*]

MACBETH [*to himself*]: One of the witches' predictions has become true. This supernatural business cannot be evil, but it cannot be good either. If it is *evil*, why has it given me a taste of success by starting with a truth? I am the Thane of Cawdor. If it is *good*, why is a horrible idea forming in my brain, which makes my heart beat fast in a most unnatural way? The thought of murder is causing my whole body to shake.

BANQUO [*to Ross and Angus, and looking at Macbeth*]: Look how thoughtful our friend is.

MACBETH [*to himself*]: If it really is my fate to be king, then it may happen without any work from me.

BANQUO: He has not got used to his new title yet.

MACBETH [*to himself*]: If it happens, it happens.

BANQUO [*calling*]: Noble Macbeth, we are waiting for you.

MACBETH: Please forgive me. I was thinking about the past. Let us go to the King. [*to Banquo*] Think about what has happened today, and let us discuss it when we have more time.

BANQUO: I will be very glad to do that.

MACBETH: Until then, let us not think about it any more. [*to Ross and Angus*] Come, friends.

[*They all leave.*]

Scene 4 An open space

[*King Duncan, Lennox, Malcolm and Donalbain enter with their attendants.*]

DUNCAN: Has the Thane of Cawdor been executed yet?

MALCOLM: My lord, the executioners have still not returned. But I spoke to someone who saw him die, who said that he died very well. He asked you to forgive him for his disloyalty, and died in such a noble way that his death became the best act of his life.

DUNCAN [*sadly*]: You cannot read a man's mind by looking at his face. I really trusted him.

[*Macbeth, Banquo, Ross and Angus enter.*]

DUNCAN [*to Macbeth*]: Oh, noble cousin! You have done so much for me. I do not know how I can ever reward you.

MACBETH: You do not need to reward me. It is enough for me to serve you and give my loyalty to you and your family.

DUNCAN: Noble Banquo, you also deserve my great thanks. [*to everyone*] Sons, relatives, thanes, and everyone who is dear to me, I am going to give all my land and property to my eldest son, Malcolm, when I die. From today, he will be known as the

Prince of Cumberland. [*to Macbeth*] Now, let us go to your castle at Inverness.

MACBETH: I will ride ahead and tell my wife that you are coming. She will be very pleased.

DUNCAN: My noble Cawdor!

MACBETH [*to himself, angrily*]: The Prince of Cumberland! So Malcolm is now in my way. I will have to solve this problem. Stars, hide your fires! I do not want light shining on my dark, secret desire to be king. [*He leaves.*]

DUNCAN [*to Banquo*]: I am very pleased with Macbeth. He is so brave, and he cannot do enough for me. Let us follow him. We have no better friend.

[*They all leave.*]

Scene 5   *The great hall in Macbeth's castle*

[*Lady Macbeth enters alone, reading a letter. She sits down at a table.*]

LADY MACBETH [*reading*]: They met me on the day of our victory, and they know things that no ordinary human beings can know. I wanted to ask them more, but they disappeared. While I stood there, shocked, messengers came from the King who called me Thane of Cawdor. The three witches greeted me with this title before they called me the future king. I wanted to tell you about these things, my dearest partner, so that you too can look forward to our great future. Keep this news in your heart, and goodbye. [*She puts the letter away in her pocket, then stands and walks around the room.*] You are Thane of Glamis, and Cawdor, and you will be king too. But I am not confident of your character; you are too full of gentle kindness to act on this opportunity. You want to be powerful, and you are ambitious, but you prefer to get what you want without harming anyone. You want to be king, but you fear what you must do. Come here quickly, so that I can give you the strength to take the crown which fate and the supernatural powers are holding out to you. [*A messenger enters.*] [*looking up*] What news do you bring?

MESSENGER: The King is coming to stay here tonight.

LADY MACBETH: You're crazy! Isn't my husband with him? Why hasn't he told me to make preparations?

MESSENGER: It really is true. Our Thane is on his way, but one of his servants rode here even faster to bring us this message.

LADY MACBETH: He brings great news. [*The messenger leaves.*] [*to herself*] So fate is leading Duncan to my castle. Come, supernatural powers, take away all my womanly qualities and make me strong and cruel from head to foot. Do not let me feel pity, or change my mind. Come, black night, and cover everything with dark smoke so that nobody will see my crime, or try to stop it. [*Macbeth enters. Lady Macbeth runs to him and throws her arms round him.*] Great Thane of Glamis, noble Thane of Cawdor! And you are going to be even greater than these! Your letter has made me forget the present. I can only think about the future.

MACBETH: My dearest love, Duncan is coming here tonight.

LADY MACBETH: And when will he leave?

MACBETH: He is planning to leave tomorrow.

LADY MACBETH: Oh, tomorrow will never come for him! But your face, my Thane, is like an open book where people can read strange things. If you want to trick people, you have to look more innocent. We must make arrangements for Duncan, and you must give me control of the important business that we have to do tonight.

MACBETH: We will discuss this later.

LADY MACBETH: Fear nothing. Leave everything to me.

[*They leave.*]

9

Scene 6   The entrance hall of Macbeth's castle

[*Duncan, Malcolm, Donalbain, Banquo, Lennox, Macduff, Ross and Angus enter with attendants.*]

DUNCAN: This castle has a very pleasant situation; the air is clean and fresh. [*Lady Macbeth enters.*] Look, our noble hostess! [*to Lady Macbeth*] My visit here is giving you a lot of trouble.

LADY MACBETH: If your visit caused us twice as much trouble, we would still not deserve it.

DUNCAN [*looking round*]: Where is the Thane of Cawdor? I tried to pass him on the road, but he is an excellent rider and his great love for you carried him here before us. Beautiful and noble hostess, I am going to be your guest tonight.

LADY MACBETH: We are your servants, and are happy to give you everything we own.

DUNCAN: Give me your hand and take me to Macbeth. I love him very much, and I will continue to reward him. [*kissing her hand*] With your permission, hostess.

[*They leave.*]

Scene 7   The great hall in Macbeth's castle

[*Servants enter and walk across the stage, carrying plates of food. Macbeth enters at the front of the stage.*]

MACBETH [*to himself*]: If this murderous act is going to end everything, it should be done quickly. Then we could jump straight from our crime into our future lives. But in a situation like this, we are never able to escape from our crime. Duncan has two reasons to trust me. First, I am his relative and he is my king, and second, I am his host. I should protect him from murderers, not carry the knife to murder him myself. In

10

addition, Duncan has performed his duties as king so well that his people will be full of grief at his death. I have no good reason to kill him except for my ambition. [*Lady Macbeth enters.*] What is happening?

LADY MACBETH [*angrily*]: He has almost finished dinner. Why did you leave the dining-room?

MACBETH: Has he asked where I am?

LADY MACBETH: Of course he has.

MACBETH: We are not going to continue with this business. Duncan has given me great rewards recently, and I am admired by many people. I do not want to lose their good opinions.

LADY MACBETH: So you were never serious about making your desires come true? Are you really so afraid? You want to have the greatest prize in life, but you act like a coward. You are like a silly cat who wants to catch a fish, but is afraid to get its feet wet.

MACBETH: Please do not say any more. I am not afraid to do anything that a man can feel proud of doing.

LADY MACBETH: So why did you tell me about this business? When you dared do it, you were a man. You had no clear opportunity then, but you wanted to do it. But now you have the perfect time and place, and you do not want to continue with it. I would prefer to kill my own child than behave in such a cowardly way.

MACBETH: But what will happen if we fail?

LADY MACBETH [*impatiently*]: Fail? Just decide to act bravely, and we will not fail. Duncan is very tired from his long journey and he will want to go to bed. When he is asleep, I will give his servants so much wine that they will get drunk and fall asleep. Then you and I can do what we like to Duncan, as he lies unprotected. Afterwards we will say that his drunken guards are guilty of his murder.

MACBETH [*admiringly*]: You are as brave as a man! So when we have marked the two drunk and sleepy guards with blood, and used

11

their daggers to murder Duncan, everyone will think that they did it?

LADY MACBETH: Who will dare say anything else, when they see how strong our grief is?

MACBETH [*with sudden decision*]: I have decided to act. Let us go and pretend to enjoy the evening. Our faces must not show the true intentions of our hearts.

[*They leave.*]

Act 2   Murder in the Castle

Scene 1   The entrance hall of Macbeth's castle

[*Banquo and Fleance enter. Fleance is carrying a lamp.*]

BANQUO: What time is it?

FLEANCE: The moon has gone down; I have not heard the clock strike.

BANQUO: The moon goes down at twelve o'clock.

FLEANCE: It must be later then.

BANQUO [*giving Fleance his sword*]: Here, take my sword. [*looking at the sky*] The night is very dark; there are no stars tonight. [*in a tired voice and stretching out his arms*] My need for rest lies on me like a heavy weight, but I do not want to sleep. When you are asleep, you dream about all kinds of terrible things. [*Macbeth enters with a servant carrying a lamp.*] [*to Fleance*] Give me my sword! [*loudly*] Who is there?

MACBETH: A friend.

BANQUO [*putting away his sword*]: Why are you not asleep yet, sir? The King is in bed. He has had an unusually good time, and is going to send you great rewards, including a diamond for your wife to thank her for her kindness as hostess.

MACBETH: We were unprepared for his visit, so we could not do as much as we wanted for him.

BANQUO: Everything was fine. [*taking Macbeth to one side*] I dreamed about the three witches last night. One of their predictions for you has come true.

MACBETH [*pretending not to be interested*]: I do not think about them. But perhaps we can discuss the subject when you have the time.

BANQUO: Of course. Whenever you like.

13

MACBETH: Fine. [*loudly*] Goodnight, and sleep well.
BANQUO: Thank you, sir; the same to you.

[*Banquo and Fleance leave.*]

MACBETH [*to his servant*]: Go and tell my wife to ring the bell
when my drink is ready. Then go to bed. [*The servant leaves.*]
[*to himself, staring into the air in front of him*] Is this a dagger
which I see in front of me, with its handle turned towards
my hand? [*trying to take hold of it*] Come, let me catch you.
I cannot hold you, but I can still see you. Can you not be
touched? Are you only a dagger of my imagination, a product
of the terrible activity in my brain? I can still see you.
[*starting to follow the dagger*] You are leading me towards
Duncan's bedroom. Either you do not exist, or my eyes are
better than my other senses. Now there are drops of blood
on you which were not there before. [*stopping suddenly*] This
dagger does not really exist. It is the idea of the bloody murder
that makes me imagine it. One half of the world is sleeping.
It is just the right time for evil crimes. [*moving forward again*]
But while I am talking, Duncan is still alive. Actions are delayed
by words. [*A bell rings.*] I am going; I will do it. The bell is
inviting me to this crime.
Duncan, do not listen to the sound of the bell.
It is calling you to Heaven or to hell.

[*He leaves.*]

Scene 2　The same entrance hall

[*Lady Macbeth enters.*]

LADY MACBETH: The wine has made the guards drunk, but it has
made me brave. [*pausing suddenly*] What was that cry? [*listening*]
It was only an owl. Macbeth is committing the murder and the

'*Macbeth is committing the murder.*'

guards are sleeping. I drugged their drinks so well that they look half alive, half dead.

MACBETH [*calling from off the stage*]: Who is there?

LADY MACBETH [*anxiously*]: I am afraid that the guards have woken up before he has managed to kill Duncan. I laid their daggers out ready; has he not seen them? I was prepared to kill Duncan myself, but he reminded me of my father as he slept. [*Macbeth enters, carrying two daggers covered with blood. Lady Macbeth runs to him.*] My husband!

MACBETH: I have done it. Did you not hear a noise?

LADY MACBETH: I heard the cry of an owl.

MACBETH [*nervously*]: Listen! [*They listen.*] Who is in the bedroom next to Duncan's?

LADY MACBETH: Donalbain.

MACBETH [*looking fearfully at his hands, which are covered in blood*]: This is a sad and terrible sight.

LADY MACBETH: This is no time for foolish thoughts.

MACBETH: One of the King's sons laughed in his sleep, and the other one shouted out, 'Murder!' They woke each other up. I stood and listened, but they soon went back to sleep. Then I thought I heard a voice cry out, 'Stop sleeping! Macbeth has murdered Sleep – innocent Sleep that takes away problems and calms hurt minds.'

LADY MACBETH: What do you mean?

MACBETH: This voice cried, 'Stop sleeping!' to everyone in the castle. 'The Thane of Glamis and Cawdor has murdered Sleep. Macbeth will never sleep again.'

LADY MACBETH [*impatiently*]: What voice cried out such things? Noble Thane, you are losing your ability to think. Get some water and wash this blood off your hands. Why did you bring these daggers out of Duncan's bedroom? They have to stay there. [*pushing him towards the room*] Go and mark the faces of the sleeping guards with blood.

MACBETH [*refusing to move*]: I am not going back into that room. I am afraid to think about what I have done. I do not dare look at it again.

LADY MACBETH [*angrily*]: How weak you are! Give me the daggers. When men are asleep or dead, they look just like pictures, nothing more. I will paint the guards' faces with Duncan's blood, because people must think that they are guilty of this crime.

[*She goes out. A loud knocking is heard from off the stage.*]

MACBETH [*nervously*]: Where is that knocking coming from? I am afraid of every noise now. [*looking at his hands*] What terrible hands! Can all the water in the wide seas wash my hands clean of blood? No, my hands would probably turn the green sea-water red.

[*Lady Macbeth enters. Her hands are also covered with blood.*]

LADY MACBETH [*showing Macbeth her hands*]: My hands are now the same colour as yours, but I would be ashamed to have such a cowardly heart. [*The loud knocking starts again.*] Someone is knocking at the south entrance. Let us go back to our room. A little water will be enough to clean away the signs of this murder. How easy it will be! [*more knocking*] Listen! More knocking. [*giving Macbeth a push*] Go and put your nightclothes on. We have to pretend we were asleep. Do not stand there, thinking.

MACBETH: If I think about this murder, I must forget the man I was. [*more knocking*] [*looking sadly towards the place where the knocking is coming from*] I am sorry that you cannot wake Duncan with your knocking!

[*They leave.*]

Scene 3   The same entrance hall

[*The loud knocking continues. A gatekeeper carrying keys enters and walks slowly across the room.*]

GATEKEEPER: What a lot of knocking! If I were the gatekeeper at the gate of hell, I would be busy all the time; there are so many people who have committed crimes. [*calling*] Who is there? [*The loud knocking continues.*] Knock, knock, knock! What do you want? [*more knocking*] But this place is too cold for hell. Who's there? [*more knocking*] All right, I'm coming.

[*He opens the gate. Macduff and Lennox enter.*]

MACDUFF: Was it so late when you went to bed, my friend, that you could not get up? Is your lord awake? [*Macbeth enters.*] Our knocking has woken him up; here he comes.

LENNOX: Good morning, noble sir.

MACBETH: Good morning to both of you.

MACDUFF: Is the King awake, noble Thane?

MACBETH: Not yet.

MACDUFF: He ordered me to come and see him early.

MACBETH: I will take you to him. [*pointing off stage*] There is the door to his room.

MACDUFF: You do not have to take me. I will go in myself.

[*He leaves.*]

LENNOX: Is the King leaving today?

MACBETH: Yes, he is.

LENNOX: The night has been very wild. The chimneys were blown away in the place where we stayed. Strange screams of death were heard in the air, warning of terrible times. Owls cried out all night, and people said that the earth shook. I cannot remember a night like it.

[*Macduff enters.*]

MACDUFF [*very shocked and upset*]: A terrible thing has happened! You cannot imagine how awful it is.

MACBETH and LENNOX: What is the matter?

MACDUFF: The King has been horribly murdered. Do not ask me to talk about it. Go to his room and see. [*Macbeth and Lennox leave. Macduff runs around the room, shouting.*] Wake up, everyone! Ring the bell! Murder! Banquo and Donalbain, Malcolm, wake up! Ring the bell!

[*The bell starts to ring. Lady Macbeth enters, wearing her nightclothes.*]

LADY MACBETH: What is happening? Why has that awful noise woken us all up? Speak, speak!

MACDUFF: Oh gentle lady, I do not know how to tell you such horrible news. [*Banquo enters.*] Oh Banquo, Banquo! The King has been murdered.

LADY MACBETH: Oh, how terrible! And in our house too!

BANQUO: It would be terrible anywhere. Please tell me it is not true, Macduff.

[*Macbeth, Lennox and Ross enter, all wearing nightclothes.*]

MACBETH [*looking very upset*]: Why did I not die an hour before this thing happened? I was a happy man then. But from this moment, all the good things in life are at an end.

[*Malcolm and Donalbain enter.*]

MALCOLM: What is wrong?

MACBETH: You have lost the most important person in your life.

MACDUFF: Your royal father has been murdered.

MALCOLM [*very shocked*]: Who did it?

LENNOX: It seems that it was the men guarding his room. Their hands and faces were all marked with blood and their daggers, also covered in blood, were lying on their pillows. They said nothing, but those men could not be trusted.

MACBETH: How sorry I am that I killed them!

MACDUFF [*shocked*]: Why did you do that?

MACBETH: Who can stay calm at such a moment? Nobody. My love for Duncan was so strong that I could not act sensibly. The King lay there, with his skin covered in blood and terrible cuts. There were the murderers with their red and bloody knives. What man, who loved his King and wanted to show his love, could stop himself from killing them?

LADY MACBETH [*fainting*]: Take me away from here!

MACDUFF [*calling off stage*]: Help the lady!

[*Two servants run in and hold Lady Macbeth up.*]

MALCOLM [*to Donalbain, quietly*]: Should we not speak out against our father's murder?

DONALBAIN [*to Malcolm, quietly*]: What can we say? This place is not safe for us. Let us escape. There is no time to show our grief.

MALCOLM [*to Donalbain*]: Or to take any action.

BANQUO [*to the servants*]: Help the lady! [*The servants take Lady Macbeth out.*] When we have got dressed, let us meet and find out more about this terrible crime. We are full of fear and doubts. But with God on my side, I will fight the traitor who carried out this terrible murder.

MACDUFF: And I!

ALL: And all of us!

MACBETH: Let us get ready quickly and meet again in the great hall.

[*Everyone leaves except Malcolm and Donalbain.*]

MALCOLM: What are you going to do? Let us not discuss anything with them. It is easy for a traitor to pretend to show sadness. I will go to England.

DONALBAIN: And I will go to Ireland. We will be safer if we are in different places. Here men may smile and appear friendly, but there are daggers behind their smiles.

MALCOLM: The best way of protecting ourselves is to leave. Let us find our horses. There is no time for long goodbyes.

[*They leave.*]

Scene 4   *The same entrance hall*

[*Ross enters with an old man.*]

OLD MAN: I am seventy years old, and I have seen some strange things in my life, but nothing as strange as last night.

ROSS: You can see how Heaven has been made angry by the murderous actions of men. It is daytime, but there is no sun. Darkness covers the earth, like night.

OLD MAN: It is against nature, like the King's unnatural death.

[*Macduff enters.*]

ROSS: Here comes Macduff. Have they found out who committed this horrible murder yet?

MACDUFF: The men that Macbeth killed.

ROSS: How terrible! But what advantage could they hope to get from such a crime?

MACDUFF: They were paid to do it. Malcolm and Donalbain, the King's two sons, have run away. So now people think that they were responsible for the murder.

ROSS: What an awful thing – to kill their father because of their ambition. So it is most likely that Macbeth will become king?

MACDUFF: He has already gone to Scone* to be crowned.

---

* Scone: a place near the town of Perth, where the Scottish kings were traditionally crowned.

ROSS: Are you going there too?

MACDUFF: No, I am going home to Fife.

ROSS: Well, I will go to Scone.

MACDUFF: I hope everything goes well there. [*to Ross, quietly*] The new king may not be as kind to us as the old one. [*loudly*] Goodbye!

ROSS [*to the old man*]: Goodbye, old man.

OLD MAN: Goodbye. May God be with you!

Act 3   The Ghost at Dinner

Scene 1   The great hall in the king's palace

[*Banquo enters.*]

BANQUO [*quietly, thoughtfully*]: You have got everything now that the three witches promised – you were Thane of Glamis, and Cawdor, and now you are King of Scotland. And I am afraid that you have committed a most terrible crime. But the witches also predicted that I, and not you, would be the father of many kings. So as their predictions have come true for you, I hope that they will also come true for me. [*Music sounds off stage.*] But Macbeth is coming. I must be silent.

[*Macbeth enters, dressed as king, with Lady Macbeth, Lennox, Ross, lords and attendants.*]

MACBETH [*walking towards Banquo*]: Here is our most important guest. Tonight, sir, we are having a very special dinner, and I want you to be there.

BANQUO: I will obey whatever you command.

MACBETH: Are you going riding this afternoon?

BANQUO: Yes, my lord.

MACBETH: Are you going far?

BANQUO: As far as I can between now and dinner.

MACBETH: Make sure that you are at the dinner.

BANQUO: My lord, I will be there.

MACBETH: I hear that Malcolm and Donalbain are in England and Ireland, spreading lies about me. But we will talk more about that tomorrow. Go and find your horse. Goodbye until tonight. [*pausing*] Is Fleance going with you?

BANQUO: Yes, my lord.

MACBETH: I hope your horses go quickly and safely. Goodbye. [*Banquo leaves.*] I want to be alone now. Let everyone do what he likes until seven o'clock this evening. Until then, God be with you!

[*Everyone starts to leave.*]

MACBETH [*calling to a servant*]: Come here. I want a word with you. [*The others continue to leave. The servant walks towards Macbeth.*] Are those men waiting for my call?

SERVANT: They are outside the palace gates, my lord.

MACBETH: Bring them in.

[*The servant leaves.*]

MACBETH: I am king now, but I still do not feel safe. I am frightened of Banquo. He has a royal quality in his character which I fear; he is very brave and wise too. The witches predicted that he would be father to a line of kings, but they did not say that my sons would be kings. Have I therefore done all these things for Banquo? Have I murdered the noble Duncan and destroyed my peace of mind so that Banquo's children can become kings? [*calling*] Who is there?

[*The servant enters with two murderers.*]

MACBETH [*to his servant*]: Now go to the door and stay there until I call you. [*The servant leaves.*] [*to the murderers*] Wasn't it yesterday when we had our discussion?

MURDERERS: Yes, my lord.

MACBETH: And have you thought about what I said? I told you that Banquo has been responsible for many things that have caused harm to you and your families. You thought that these things were my fault, but they were Banquo's.

FIRST MURDERER: You told us that, my lord.

MACBETH: I did, and now I want to know what you are going to do about it. Do you have such kind natures that you can let this man go unpunished? [*pausing*] If you want to get rid of him, I will arrange an opportunity for you to kill him.

SECOND MURDERER: I've suffered so much, my lord, and become so angry, that I don't care what I do now.

FIRST MURDERER: Me too. I'm so tired of problems that I'll take any opportunity to improve my life.

MACBETH: Both of you know that Banquo was your enemy.

MURDERERS: That's true, my lord.

MACBETH: Well, he's my enemy too. But if I used my power as king to get rid of him openly, I would lose the support of many important people who are his friends. So I am asking for your help. This business has to be secret; I don't want the whole world to know about it.

SECOND MURDERER: We'll do as you command.

FIRST MURDERER: Even if we die.

MACBETH: Good. I'll tell you within an hour exactly where to position yourselves, and when. This thing has to be done tonight, and some distance from the palace so that I am completely free from suspicion. Fleance, Banquo's son, must die at the same time.

MURDERERS: We'll do it, my lord.

MACBETH: I'll come to you immediately. Go and wait for me. [*The murderers leave.*] It is finished! Banquo, tonight you will be on your way to Heaven!

[*He leaves.*]

Scene 2   *Lady Macbeth's room in the palace*

[*Lady Macbeth and a servant enter.*]

LADY MACBETH: Has Banquo left the castle?
SERVANT: Yes, but he's coming back tonight.

25

LADY MACBETH: Ask the King to come and see me.

SERVANT: Yes, madam. [*The servant leaves.*]

LADY MACBETH: We have done everything, but we have won nothing. We have got what we wanted, but we are not happy. [*Macbeth enters. She goes towards him lovingly.*] Why do you stay by yourself, thinking sad thoughts about the past? Do not waste time thinking about things that cannot be changed.

MACBETH [*pushing her away*]: We are still not out of danger. I cannot eat and I have terrible dreams at night. I would prefer to die than continue to suffer these fears. Duncan is dead; he is at peace after the troubles of life. His suffering has ended and nothing can touch him now.

LADY MACBETH: Please, my lord, take that unpleasant look off your face. Be happy and welcoming to your guests tonight.

MACBETH [*trying to look happy*]: I will, my love, and you must too. Remember to give special attention to Banquo. These times are so unsafe that we must not allow our faces to show the true feelings of our hearts.

LADY MACBETH: You must stop thinking about these things.

MACBETH: My mind is full of dangerous thoughts, dear wife! You know that Banquo and Fleance are still alive. But before night, a terrible crime will take place.

LADY MACBETH [*surprised*]: What is going to happen?

MACBETH: It is better that you do not know about it now. But when you do know, you will be glad. [*looking out of the window*] It is beginning to get dark. The good creatures of day are beginning to feel sleepy, but the creatures of night are starting to wake up and go hunting. You are surprised at my words, but be patient. Things with evil beginnings grow stronger through more evil. [*holding out his hand*] Please, come with me.

[*They leave.*]

Scene 3 *A dark road with trees outside the palace*

[*The three murderers enter. They are arguing.*]

FIRST MURDERER [*to the third murderer, suspiciously*]: But who ordered you to join us?

THIRD MURDERER: Macbeth.

SECOND MURDERER: Doesn't he trust us? He told us exactly what we have to do.

FIRST MURDERER [*to the third murderer*]: Well, stand here with us. There's still a little bit of light in the sky. Our man can't be far away now.

THIRD MURDERER: Listen, I can hear horses!

BANQUO [*calling from off stage*]: Give us a light!

SECOND MURDERER: There! That's him!

FIRST MURDERER: His horses are going away.

THIRD MURDERER: People usually walk from here to the palace gates.

[*The three murderers hide behind some trees. Banquo and Fleance enter. Fleance is carrying a lamp.*]

SECOND MURDERER [*whispering*]: A light! A light!

THIRD MURDERER: It's him!

FIRST MURDERER: Get ready!

BANQUO: It's going to rain tonight.

FIRST MURDERER [*jumping out at him*]: Yes, with blood!

[*All the murderers jump out and attack Banquo.*]

BANQUO: Oh, I have been betrayed! Run, Fleance, run!

[*Banquo is cut down and falls. Fleance escapes, taking the lamp.*]

THIRD MURDERER: Where's the light gone? We've killed only one of them; the son's escaped.

SECOND MURDERER: We've lost half our reward.

FIRST MURDERER: Well, let's go immediately and report what's happened.

[*They leave.*]

Scene 4   *The great hall in the King's palace*

[*Macbeth, Lady Macbeth, Ross, Lennox, lords and attendants enter. The table has been laid for dinner.*]

MACBETH: Welcome, everybody! You all know your places. Please sit down.

LORDS: Thank you.

[*The attendants show the lords and Lady Macbeth to their seats.*]

MACBETH: I will move around among you like a good host. [*walking around the table*] Your hostess welcomes you too.

LADY MACBETH: Welcome, dear friends, with all my heart.

[*The first murderer enters and stands on one side of the stage.*]

MACBETH [*to Lady Macbeth*]: See how everybody thanks you. [*sitting down in the middle of one side of the table*] I will sit here in the middle. Be happy, everyone. Let us all have a drink.

[*The attendants bring drink and the lords and Lady Macbeth talk among themselves. Macbeth suddenly sees the murderer. He gets up and walks towards him.*]

MACBETH: There's blood on your face!

FIRST MURDERER: It's Banquo's blood.

MACBETH: Is he dead?

FIRST MURDERER: My lord, I cut his throat.

MACBETH: Excellent! But what about Fleance? Did you do the same for him?

FIRST MURDERER [*nervously*]: My lord, Fleance escaped.

MACBETH [*to himself, fearfully*]: Now all my doubts and fears are returning. [*to the murderer*] But Banquo's dead?

FIRST MURDERER: Yes, my lord. His body's lying in a hole in the ground, with twenty deep cuts on the head. He is certainly dead.

MACBETH: Thank you for that. [*to himself*] The father is dead. The son has escaped and will be dangerous one day, but for the present time, he has no power to attack me. [*to the murderer*] Now go. I'll hear more about this tomorrow.

[*The murderer leaves.*]

LADY MACBETH [*to Macbeth, calling*]: My lord, you are forgetting your guests.

MACBETH: Thank you for reminding me. [*lifting a cup*] Your happiness and good health, everyone!

LENNOX: Please come and sit down, sir.

[*The ghost of Banquo, covered with blood, enters behind Macbeth and sits down in Macbeth's place at the table. Macbeth does not see the ghost.*]

MACBETH [*standing and holding the cup*]: All the greatest men in Scotland are under my roof tonight, except noble Banquo. It is very rude of him not to come.

ROSS: He must be blamed for not keeping his promise. Would you like to come and sit with us, my royal lord?

MACBETH [*looking at the table*]: But the table is full.

LENNOX: We have kept a place for you here, sir.

MACBETH: Where?

LENNOX: Here, my lord. [*surprised*] What is the matter?

[*Macbeth sees the ghost and steps back in terror, dropping his cup of drink on the floor.*]

MACBETH [*looking round fearfully*]: Which one of you has done this?

LORDS [*very surprised*]: What, sir?

MACBETH [*to the ghost*]: You cannot say I murdered you; do not shake your bloody head at me.

ROSS: Gentlemen, get up. [*The guests stand.*] The King is ill.

[*Lady Macbeth leaves her chair and walks towards Macbeth.*]

LADY MACBETH [*to the lords*]: Sit down, noble friends. [*They sit.*] My husband often acts in this strange way, and has done since he was a young man. Please stay in your seats. This mad behaviour will pass very quickly. Do not take any notice of him. [*to Macbeth, quietly and angrily*] Act like a man!

MACBETH: I am not brave enough to look at that thing from hell!

LADY MACBETH [*more angrily*]: What foolishness! You are always seeing things that do not exist, like daggers in the air. You should be ashamed. Why are you so afraid? It is only an empty chair that you are looking at.

MACBETH: Please, look at it! Look! [*The ghost moves its head up and down.*] [*to the ghost, fearfully*] What do you want to say? Speak!

[*The ghost leaves.*]

LADY MACBETH: You cowardly fool!

MACBETH: I saw him as clearly as I am standing here. In the past, when men died violent deaths, that was the end of them. But now, a dead man comes back again with cuts all over his head and pushes me out of my chair.

LADY MACBETH [*loudly*]: My lord, you must give your noble friends your attention.

MACBETH [*to the lords, trying to be welcoming*]: I am very sorry. I forgot. Do not be surprised about my behaviour, dear friends. I suffer from an unusual illness, which my closest friends and family do not take any notice of. [*lifting a cup*] Love and health

'Which one of you has done this?'

to everyone! I will sit down. Fill my cup with wine. [*An attendant brings wine to Macbeth. The ghost enters behind Macbeth so that Macbeth does not see it.*] I will drink to the happiness of everyone here, and especially to my dear friend Banquo, who I miss very much.

LORDS [*lifting their cups*]: To Banquo!

MACBETH [*suddenly seeing the ghost and dropping his cup*]: Get out of my sight! You are no living creature.

LADY MACBETH [*to the lords*]: Noble lords, please do not think that my husband's behaviour is strange, although it does spoil our enjoyment of our dinner.

MACBETH [*to the ghost*]: I am as brave as any man. If you came to me in the shape of a wild animal – in any shape except the one you have – I would not be afraid. If you were alive and dared me to fight, I would. Get out of here, you horrible shadow! [*The ghost leaves. The lords start to get up.*] Now it has gone, and I can act like a man again. [*to the lords*] Please sit down.

LADY MACBETH [*with quiet anger*]: You have spoiled everyone's enjoyment and destroyed the happy mood with your strange madness.

MACBETH [*to the lords*]: Can such things really happen, to take away our pleasure like a black cloud in summer? How can you see such horrible sights and not turn pale with fear, like me?

ROSS [*in surprised disbelief*]: What sights, my lord?

LADY MACBETH: Do not say anything to him; he is becoming worse and worse. Questions will only make him angry. Now, goodnight. [*The lords still wait.*] [*losing her calm*] Do not wait for my husband to leave first; just go.

LENNOX [*coming forward to kiss her hand*]: Goodnight. I hope the King feels better soon.

LADY MACBETH: Goodnight.

[*Everyone leaves except Macbeth and Lady Macbeth.*]

MACBETH [*still fearful*]: It wants blood, my blood. [*pausing*] What time is it?

LADY MACBETH: It is almost morning.

MACBETH: Macduff was not present at our dinner tonight. What do you think that means?

LADY MACBETH: Have you sent for him?

MACBETH: No, but I will tomorrow. I pay a servant in every castle to tell me what is going on. I will soon find out what he is doing. And I will also go and see the three witches. I want them to tell me more. I have committed so many bloody crimes now that I cannot return to the person I used to be. I have so many strange thoughts in my head.

LADY MACBETH [*anxiously*]: You need to sleep.

MACBETH [*holding out his hand*]: Come, let us go to bed. I have many things to do tomorrow.

[*They leave.*]

Scene 5 *The same great hall in the palace*

[*Lennox and Ross enter.*]

LENNOX: You and I are sharing the same thoughts. Noble Duncan and brave Banquo are dead. You can say, if you like, that Fleance killed Banquo, because Fleance ran away. And everyone agrees how shocking it was for Malcolm and Donalbain to kill their father. [*pausing, then shaking his head*] Macbeth was most upset by this evil crime. Did he not immediately kill the two drunken criminals before they could say that they were innocent? If he catches Duncan's sons – and I really hope he will not – he will punish them, and Fleance too. [*changing the subject*] But I hear that Macbeth is angry with Macduff, because Macduff did not come to this tyrant's dinner. Do you know where Macduff is?

ROSS: Malcolm was Duncan's son, but the tyrant took away his right to be king. Malcolm is staying in England with good King Edward, who has welcomed him with great kindness. And Macduff has gone to England too, to ask Edward for help. He wants Edward to order the powerful English lord, Seyward, to bring an army against Macbeth and free Scotland from these unhappy times of danger and suspicion. Then we can live freely and in peace again.

LENNOX: Did Macbeth order Macduff to come and see him?

LORD: Yes, but Macduff refused to come.

LENNOX: I hope that he travels to England very fast, so that the sufferings of our country will soon be ended!

[*They leave.*]

Act 4   Death of the Innocents

Scene 1   An open place in the forest

[*A large black pot is hanging over a fire. The three witches enter to the sound of thunder. They dance around the pot.*]

FIRST WITCH: Round and round the pot we go,
Sometimes fast and sometimes slow.
ALL [*dancing*]: Double, double, pain and trouble,
Fire burn and water bubble!
SECOND WITCH: Make sure the fire is good and hot,
Throw magic things into the pot.
ALL [*throwing things in*]: Double, double, pain and trouble,
Fire burn and water bubble!
THIRD WITCH: Boil the magic drink for longer,
Then its power will be much stronger!
ALL [*looking into pot as they dance*]:
Double, double, pain and trouble,
Fire burn and water bubble!
SECOND WITCH [*stopping suddenly*]:
I feel a sharp pain in my thumbs,
Something very evil comes!

[*Macbeth enters.*]

MACBETH: Greetings, evil old women of the night! What kind of magic are you making?
ALL: A kind that has no name.
MACBETH: I command you to answer my questions.
FIRST WITCH: Speak!
SECOND WITCH: Ask!
THIRD WITCH: We'll show you the answers. Watch!

[*They throw more things into the pot. A soldier dressed in armour enters and walks across the stage.*]

MACBETH [*to the soldier*]: Tell me –

FIRST WITCH: He knows what you want to ask. Listen to him but don't say anything.

SOLDIER: Macbeth, Macbeth, Macbeth, be careful of Macduff! Be careful of the Thane of Fife!

[*He leaves.*]

MACBETH: Whatever you are, thank you for this warning. You guessed correctly what I was afraid of. But one thing more –

FIRST WITCH: You can't tell him what to do. But here's someone else, more powerful than the first.

[*A child, covered in blood, enters and walks across the stage.*]

CHILD: Macbeth, Macbeth, Macbeth! Be brave and strong! You can laugh at the power of men. Macbeth can't be harmed by any man born from a woman!

[*The child leaves.*]

MACBETH: Then you can live, Macduff; I don't have to be afraid of you. But I'd better kill you, just to make sure.

[*A child with a crown on his head, and a tree in his hand, enters and walks across the stage to the sound of thunder.*]

MACBETH: What's this thing, which looks like a king?

SECOND WITCH: Listen, but don't speak to it.

CHILD: Be strong and brave, and don't worry. Macbeth will never be beaten until Birnam Wood marches against him to Dunsinane Hill. [*He leaves.*]

MACBETH [*pleased*]: That can never happen. Who can control the forest and make the trees move? Good! These are excellent predictions! But I'm very anxious to know one more thing. Tell me if Banquo's children will be kings of Scotland.

THIRD WITCH: Don't ask any more questions.

MACBETH: I have to know the answer!

FIRST WITCH [*calling*]: Appear!

SECOND WITCH: Appear!

THIRD WITCH: Appear!

ALL: Appear to him and grieve his heart,
Come like shadows, then depart.

[*Eight kings enter, and walk slowly in a line across the stage.*]

MACBETH [*frightened, to the first king*]: You look too much like Banquo's ghost. [*to the witches*] Why are you showing me these things, you ugly old women? The second and third kings look like the first. Now there's a fourth one too … does this line of kings never end? There's a seventh, and an eighth. I don't want to see any more. [*The ghost of Banquo enters, smiling and pointing to the line of kings. The ghost follows the kings across the stage.*] What a horrible sight! Now I see that this will really happen. There's Banquo, his hair covered in blood, smiling and pointing. Are they his children? Is it true?

FIRST WITCH: Yes, sir, everything is true. But why does it surprise you? [*to the other witches*] Come, sisters …
Fill the air with magic sound,
And for Macbeth we'll dance around!

[*Music plays off stage. The witches dance and disappear.*]

MACBETH: Where have they gone? [*He goes to the side of the stage and calls.*] Come here!

[*Lennox enters.*]

LENNOX: What can I do for you, my lord?

MACBETH: Did you see the three witches?

LENNOX [*surprised*]: No, my lord.

MACBETH: Did they not pass you?

LENNOX: No, my lord.

MACBETH: If anyone trusts them, let him go to hell. I heard some horses. Who has arrived?

LENNOX: Some gentlemen, my lord, who have come to tell you that Macduff has run away to England.

MACBETH: Run away to England!

LENNOX: Yes, my noble lord.

MACBETH [*to himself*]: I must act without delay. I will attack Macduff's castle in a surprise attack, take his lands and kill his wife and children. I will do this thing before I can change my mind. [*to Lennox*] Where are these gentlemen? Take me to them!

[*They leave.*]

Scene 2   *Macduff's castle*

[*Lady Macduff, her son and Ross enter.*]

LADY MACDUFF [*very upset*]: What terrible thing did my husband do, that made him run away from Scotland?

ROSS: You must be patient, madam.

LADY MACDUFF: *He* was not patient. It was mad of him to run away. Now everybody will think that he was a traitor.

ROSS: Perhaps he acted wisely.

LADY MACDUFF: Was it wise to leave his wife, children and home in a country which he has left? He cannot love us. Even small birds fight to defend their families against attacks by owls.

ROSS: Please be sensible, cousin. Your husband is wise and noble and understands these troubled times very well. I do not dare say much more. But these times are very cruel, when we can be traitors and not know why.

LADY MACDUFF [*looking at her son*]: He has a father, but his father has left him.

ROSS: I have to go now. [*He leaves.*]

LADY MACDUFF [*to her son*]: Your father's dead. What will you do now? How will you manage without a father?

SON: I'll look after myself, like birds do. But I don't believe my father's dead. If he were dead, you would be crying.

[*A messenger runs in.*]

MESSENGER [*shocked and upset*]: God be with you, madam! You do not know me, but I have come to warn you that you are in danger. If you will take my advice, leave here at once with your children. I do not mean to frighten you. May Heaven protect you! I dare not stay any longer. [*He leaves quickly.*]

LADY MACDUFF: Where should I run to? I have done no wrong. But in this world, rewards are often given to evil people, while good people are thought to be mad. [*The three murderers enter with swords in their hands.*] Who are you?

FIRST MURDERER: Where's your husband?

LADY MACDUFF: I hope he is in a place where men like you can never find him.

SECOND MURDERER: He's a traitor!

SON: You're lying!

THIRD MURDERER: What, you little rat!

[*He takes out his knife and pushes it into the son.*]

SON: He's killed me, Mother! Run away! [*He dies.*]

LADY MACDUFF [*screaming*]: Murder! [*She runs out, followed by the three murderers.*]

'You're lying!'

Scene 3   A room in King Edward's palace in England

[*Malcolm and Macduff enter.*]

MACDUFF: Our poor country is suffering greatly under this evil tyrant, Macbeth.

MALCOLM: Every day more terrible things happen here.

MACDUFF: Oh, Scotland! When will you see happy days again?

[*Ross enters.*]

MACDUFF: Look who is here! Welcome, cousin. Are things still the same in Scotland?

ROSS: There is no happiness in our poor country, only sad acts of violence. There is no place for good people. [*to Malcolm*] We need your help now. There are many people who are ready and willing to fight against Macbeth.

MALCOLM: We are coming. Noble King Edward has lent me brave Lord Seyward and ten thousand soldiers. There is no wiser and more experienced soldier than he is.

ROSS: That *is* good news. But I have something terrible to say, which will mainly affect you, Macduff.

MACDUFF: Then tell me quickly.

ROSS: It is the worst news you have ever heard. [*very sadly*] Your castle was attacked, and your wife and children were cruelly murdered.

MACDUFF [*completely shocked*]: My children too?

ROSS: Your wife, children and servants – everyone.

MACDUFF: Oh, why was I not there! My wife was killed too?

ROSS: Yes.

MACDUFF [*crying*]: All my children? Did you say *all*? *All* my little ones and their mother, all at once?

MALCOLM: You must take this bad news like a man.

MACDUFF: I will. But I must also *feel* it like a man, when I think

41

about the people who were dearest to me. How could Heaven let this terrible thing happen? Evil Macbeth! You arranged it because you wanted to punish me.

MALCOLM: Let your grief turn to anger and harden your heart.

MACDUFF: I will meet this tyrant of Scotland face to face, and push the length of my sword through his body.

MALCOLM: Now you are talking like a man. Come, let us go to King Edward. Our army is prepared; we only have to say goodbye. We are ready to attack Macbeth.

[*They all leave.*]

Act 5   The Moving Forest

Scene 1   A room in the King's palace

[*A doctor and Lady Macbeth's servant enter.*]

DOCTOR: Are you sure that she walks in her sleep?

SERVANT: I've watched her get out of bed, take out paper, write something and return to bed – all while she's asleep.

DOCTOR: What have you heard her say?

SERVANT: I daren't tell you, since I have no witness to her words. [*Lady Macbeth enters, dressed in her nightclothes and carrying a lamp.*] Look, here she comes! She's asleep.

DOCTOR: Where did she get that lamp from?

SERVANT: It was by her bed. She always has a light beside her. Those are her orders.

[*Lady Macbeth puts the lamp down, then starts to rub her hands together.*]

DOCTOR: Her eyes are open. What's she doing? See how she rubs her hands.

SERVANT: That's what she usually does – she seems to be washing them. I've seen her do it for fifteen minutes.

LADY MACBETH [*to herself*]: There is still a spot of blood here. Disappear, spot! Are you afraid, my husband, although you are a soldier? But who could imagine that the old man had so much blood inside him?

DOCTOR [*to the servant, shocked*]: Did you hear that?

LADY MACBETH: Macduff, the Thane of Fife, had a wife. But where is she now? Oh, will these hands never be clean?

SERVANT: She has said things which she should not say.

LADY MACBETH: My hands still smell of blood. All the perfumes of Arabia will not sweeten this little hand. [*crying*] Oh! Oh! Oh!

DOCTOR: What a terrible cry! Her heart is very troubled. I have no cure for this illness.

LADY MACBETH: Wash your hands, put on your nightclothes, do not look so pale. Banquo is dead; he cannot come back.

DOCTOR [*very shocked*]: I understand now!

LADY MACBETH: To bed, to bed! [*putting out her hand to an imaginary person*] Come, give me your hand. We cannot change things which have happened. [*She leaves.*]

DOCTOR: She needs help from a minister of religion more than a doctor. Look after her, and take away anything she can hurt herself with. I dare not say what I am thinking. Goodnight.

SERVANT: Goodnight, doctor.

[*They leave.*]

Scene 2   *An open place in the country*

[*Angus, Lennox, Cathness and Menteth enter with soldiers.*]

MENTETH: The English army is very near. Malcolm is leading it with Lord Seyward and good Macduff.

ANGUS: We will meet them near Birnam Wood.

MENTETH: What is the tyrant Macbeth doing?

CATHNESS: He is strengthening his castle at Dunsinane. Some people think he is mad.

ANGUS: The soldiers in his army obey him only because it is their duty, not because they love him. Now he is finding out that his title has no value because he got it through crime.

MENTETH: He knows that he has acted in an evil way.

CATHNESS: Well, let us continue.

LENNOX: Yes, let us march on to Birnam.

[*They all leave.*]

'All the perfumes of Arabia will not sweeten this little hand.'

Scene 3 The great hall of the King's palace

[*Macbeth enters with the doctor and attendants.*]

MACBETH: Do not bring me any more reports about the thanes running away. I will never be afraid until Birnam Wood comes to Dunsinane. And was the boy Malcolm not born from a woman? The witches told me that no man born from a woman can ever harm me. So let the false thanes run away and join the English. I will never be afraid. [*A servant enters.*] [*impatiently*] Go to hell, you fool! Why do you look so pale?

SERVANT [*fearfully*]: There are ten thousand soldiers, sir.

MACBETH: What soldiers, you cowardly boy?

SERVANT: The English army.

MACBETH: Get out of here! [*The servant leaves.*] [*calling*] Seyton! [*to himself*] I have lived long enough now. But I do not have the things which should come with old age – love and lots of loyal friends. Instead, people secretly hate me. Seyton!

[*Seyton enters.*]

SEYTON: What can I do for you, my lord?

MACBETH: Is there any more news?

SEYTON: All the reports about the English army are true.

MACBETH: I will fight until my skin is cut from my bones. Bring me my armour.

SEYTON: You do not need it yet, sir.

MACBETH: I will put it on. I want to be prepared. Send out more men on horses to find out what is happening. [*to his attendants*] Bring me my armour. [*Two attendants hurry from the room.*] [*to the doctor*] How is your patient, doctor?

DOCTOR [*nervously*]: Her illness is more an illness of the mind than of the body. She is imagining a lot of things which keep her from sleep.

MACBETH: Can you not cure a person with a sick mind?

DOCTOR: She is the only person who can cure herself.

MACBETH: All medicine is useless! [*The attendants return with armour.*] Come, help me put my armour on. [*They help him.*] Seyton, send out the horses. Doctor, the thanes are leaving me. If you could rid Scotland of this disease from England, I would be very pleased. Have you heard about the English army?

DOCTOR: Yes, my lord.

MACBETH: I will not be afraid of death until Birnam Wood comes to Dunsinane. [*He leaves.*]

DOCTOR [*to himself*]: If I were far away from Dunsinane, I would not return here for all the money in the world.

Scene 4   A forest

[*A drum sounds. Malcolm, Seyward, Macduff, Menteth, Cathness and Angus enter with soldiers marching. The soldiers form a line across the stage.*]

SEYWARD: What is this wood called?

MENTETH: Birnam Wood.

MALCOLM [*to the soldiers*]: Each of you must cut down a tree and carry it in front of you. In this way we will hide the true number of soldiers in our army from the enemy.

SOLDIERS: We will do it. [*They begin to cut down trees.*]

SEYWARD: We have heard that the tyrant Macbeth is still in Dunsinane, and intends to stay there.

MALCOLM: It is the best thing he can do. Many of his men left him when they had an opportunity.

MACDUFF: Let us make our judgements after we have fought him.

SEYWARD: Yes, the future will only be made clear through battle. [*to the soldiers*] Let us march on!

[*The soldiers form a line and they all leave, marching.*]

Scene 5 The great hall of the King's palace

[*Macbeth enters with Seyton and soldiers to the sound of a drum.*]

MACBETH: Hang our flags from the walls. Our castle is strong and the enemy will not be able to break it down. Many of my men have joined the other side and so I have lost their support. But with them, I could beat these English easily. [*Women's cries are heard off stage.*] What was that noise?

SEYTON: It was the cry of women, my lord. [*He leaves.*]

MACBETH [*to himself*]: I have almost forgotten what it is like to be afraid. I have seen so many terrible things. [*Seyton enters.*] What was that cry?

SEYTON [*sadly*]: The Queen, my lord, is dead. She has killed herself.

MACBETH [*with no emotion*]: Well, she had to die sometime. [*to himself*] All our tomorrows take us slowly towards death. And all our yesterdays, too, have only shown us the way there. Life is like a walking shadow, like an actor who performs on stage for a short time, and then is never heard again. It is like a story told by a fool, full of noise and emotion, but meaning nothing. [*A messenger enters.*] What is it? Quickly!

MESSENGER [*nervously*]: My noble lord, I do not know how to tell you what I saw.

MACBETH [*impatiently*]: Well, tell me!

MESSENGER: As I looked towards Birnam, I thought I saw the forest move.

MACBETH [*in angry disbelief*]: You are lying!

MESSENGER: It is true. You can see it. It is a moving forest.

MACBETH: If you are lying, I will hang you from the nearest tree. [*to himself*] If you are telling the truth, you can do the same for me. The witches told me, 'Don't be afraid until Birnam Wood comes to Dunsinane,' and now a wood is coming to Dunsinane. If this man is right, everything is finished. There is no reason to

'I thought I saw the forest move.'

try to escape or to stay here. I am beginning to be very tired of life. I just want everything to end. [*loudly*] Ring the bell! Let the wind blow and the storm do its worst! At least I will die fighting!

[*They all leave.*]

Scene 6   The same hall in the King's palace

[*Macbeth enters.*]

MACBETH: I have nowhere to escape to. I must stay and fight. But I will only fear a man who was not born from a woman.

[*An English soldier enters.*]

SOLDIER: What is your name?
MACBETH: If I tell you, you will be afraid.
SOLDIER: No, I will not.
MACBETH: My name is Macbeth. Now you are afraid.
SOLDIER: You are lying! I will kill you with my sword and prove it!

[*They fight and Macbeth kills the soldier.*]

MACBETH: You were born from a woman so it was easy to kill you! [*He leaves.*]

[*Macduff enters, holding his sword.*]

MACDUFF [*calling*]: Tyrant, come out, wherever you are. If somebody else kills you, and not me, the ghosts of my wife and children will never leave me in peace. [*to himself*] I must find him. [*He leaves.*]

[*Malcolm and Seyward enter.*]

SEYWARD: This way, my lord. We have taken the castle without using much force, and victory is almost ours.

[*They leave. Macbeth enters with his sword.*]

MACBETH: I am not going to kill myself like the foolish Romans used to do when they lost a battle.

[*Macduff enters and sees Macbeth.*]

MACDUFF: Turn, you dog from hell, turn!

MACBETH: Get away from me! I have murdered too many people from your family already.

MACDUFF: There is nothing I want to say to you. [*taking out his sword*] Let my sword speak for me.

[*They fight. Macbeth starts to win.*]

MACBETH: You cannot harm me. My life is protected. No man can hurt me unless he was not born from a woman.

MACDUFF: Then listen to this! I was not born naturally. I was cut from my mother's body.

MACBETH [*realising that everything is finished*]: Now I see that I cannot believe the witches' words. They have played with me and spoken with double meanings. They seemed to promise me everything, but they have broken their promises. [*putting down his sword*] I will not fight with you any more.

MACDUFF: Then surrender, coward! I will fix your head on a long stick and write underneath, 'Look at the tyrant!'

MACBETH [*picking up his sword again*]: I will not surrender so that I have to kiss the ground under the boy Malcolm's feet, in front of an angry crowd. Birnam Wood has come to Dunsinane, and you are a man who was not born from a woman, but I will fight you to the end. Come on, Macduff, do your worst!

[*They fight, and Macbeth is killed. Macduff pulls Macbeth's body off the stage. Malcolm, Seyward, Ross and the other thanes and soldiers enter.*]

51

SEYWARD: We have lost very few men today.
MALCOLM: But Macduff is missing.

[*Macduff enters with Macbeth's head.*]

MACDUFF [*to Malcolm*]: Hail, King! That is your title now. Here is the tyrant's head. Now we are free again. [*going down on his knees*] Hail, King of Scotland!
ALL [*going down on their knees*]: Hail, King of Scotland!
MALCOLM: Friends and relatives, we must first call home to Scotland all those people who escaped from this dead murderer and his evil queen. I thank every one of you, and invite you all to see me crowned at Scone.

[*They all get up and leave.*]

ACTIVITIES

Act 1

Before you read

1 Macbeth is one of Shakespeare's most famous characters. Name three other Shakespearean characters. What plays are they from?

2 Look at the Word List at the back of the book. Check the meaning of unfamiliar words, then talk to another student.

   a Who do you always trust? Has anyone ever betrayed you?

   b *Macbeth* contains witches who can predict the future. What is your favourite story about witches? Tell the story.

While you read

3 Who is being talked about? Write the answer.

   a '*He* cut *him* open from his chin to his stomach.'

     ....

   b '*Your* children will be kings.'

     ....

   c '*They* have disappeared like breath in the wind.'

     ....

   d 'The thought of murder is causing *my* whole body to shake.'

     ....

   e 'Make *me* strong and cruel from head to foot.'

     ....

   f 'Tomorrow will never come for *him*!'

     ....

After you read

4 Are these statements true or false? Correct the false ones.

   a The Thane of Cawdor helps Macbeth win the battle.

   b The witches predict that Banquo will be king.

   c King Duncan's castle is in Inverness.

   d Lady Macbeth is very pleased about Duncan's visit.

5 Answer these questions.

   a Why doesn't Macbeth believe the witches' predictions at first? Why does he change his mind?

   b What does Lady Macbeth feel about her husband's character?

53

Acts 2 and 3

Before you read

6 Do you think that Macbeth will really carry out the plan to kill
   Duncan? Discuss these questions.
   a What problems will he face if Duncan dies tonight?
   b What will Banquo think?

While you read

7 Number these events in the correct order, from 1 to 8.
   a Macbeth is crowned king.   .....
   b Duncan is murdered.   .....
   c Macduff leaves the country.   .....
   d Banquo is killed.   .....
   e Macduff's wife and children are killed.   .....
   f Duncan's sons escape.   .....
   g Duncan's guards are killed.   .....
   h Banquo's son escapes.   .....

After you read

8 Discuss these questions.
   a How do these people feel after the murder of Duncan?
      Macbeth   Lady Macbeth   Banquo   Macduff
      Malcolm and Donalbain
   b Why does Macbeth decide to kill Banquo and Fleance? How
      does he arrange this?
9 Work with another student. You are two lords who were guests at
   Macbeth's dinner. Discuss Macbeth's strange behaviour. How can
   you explain it?

Acts 4 and 5

Before you read

10 Discuss these questions.
   a What would you do now if you were Macbeth? Is there any way
      he can go back to his old life?
   b Is Macbeth wise to go and see the three witches again? Do you
      think that he can trust their predictions?

11 Are these statements true (T) or false (F)?

    a Lady Macbeth walks and talks while she is asleep.   .....

    b Her hands are covered in blood.   .....

    c Macbeth is loved by his soldiers.   .....

    d He wants to die.   .....

    e A forest of trees marches to Dunsinane.   .....

    f Macduff's mother gave birth without a doctor's help.   .....

    g Malcolm becomes king.   .....

After you read

12 Which of these characters' deaths was Macbeth responsible for? Which is the only character who doesn't die?

    Banquo   The Thane of Cawdor   Duncan   Lady Macduff

    Lady Macbeth   Fleance

13 Discuss what murder did to the minds of Macbeth and Lady Macbeth.

Writing

14 What were the witches' predictions for Macbeth? Were they correct? How did they trick him with hidden meanings?

15 How do you feel about Macbeth at the end of the play? What were his good and bad qualities?

16 Write about the importance of one of these people to the story.

    Lady Macbeth   Banquo   Macduff

17 Write a letter from King Malcolm to Fleance inviting him to return to Scotland. Tell him what has happened to Macbeth.

WORD LIST

ambition (n) a strong desire to be successful or powerful

armour (n) metal or leather clothing that men used to wear in battle

battle (n) a fight between two armies

betray (v) to behave disloyally to someone

bubble (v) to produce balls of air in a liquid

commit (v) to do something wrong or illegal

creature (n) an animal, or a person that you strongly dislike

crown (n/v) a circle of gold and jewels which kings and queens wear on their heads

dagger (n) a short, pointed knife, used in fights

evil (n/adj) something very bad, with a cruel or harmful effect

execute (v) to kill someone as a punishment for a crime

fate (n) a power that controls what happens in people's lives

grief (n) extreme sadness, especially after someone has died

hail (v) to greet someone that you admire

moor (n) an area of rough land covered with grass or other low plants

noble (adj) good or admired; of the highest social class

owl (n) a bird with large eyes and a loud call that hunts at night

perfume (n) a liquid with a strong, pleasant smell

predict (v) to say that something will happen

rub (v) to move your hand over something while you press against it

supernatural (adj) impossible to explain by science or natural causes

surrender (v) to announce that you have stopped fighting because you can't win

suspicion (n) a feeling that someone has done something wrong

sword (n) a long, sharp knife that was used in battle

traitor (n) someone who is disloyal to their country or friends

trust (v) to believe that someone will not lie to you or harm you

truth (n) the true facts about something

tyrant (n) someone who uses their power cruelly and unfairly

victory (n) the winning of a battle

witch (n) a woman who has magic powers, especially to do bad things